Beowulf

A Rock Musical

Ken Pickering and Keith Cole

Samuel French—London
New York – Sydney – Toronto – Hollywood

ISBN 978-0-573-08052-4

www.samuelfrench.co.uk
www.samuelfrench.com

FOR AMATEUR PRODUCTION ENQUIRIES

UNITED KINGDOM AND WORLD
EXCLUDING NORTH AMERICA
plays@samuelfrench.co.uk
020 7255 4302/01

Each title is subject to availability from Samuel French,
depending upon country of performance.

BEOWULF

This musical was first performed in April, 1981 by the pupils of Chesham High School, Bucks and in July, 1981 by Performing Arts students of Nonington College, Dover.

CHARACTERS

Hrothgar, King of Danes
His Queen
Hygd, their daughter
Obe, a jester – who fixes a lot of things
A Minstrel
Beowulf, a Great Champion
Hunferth Hairy Legs, a wrestler
Grendel, a slimy punk in full bondage
Grendel's Mother, a she-monster
Hammerfist, a blacksmith
A Priest
Brunhilde
Hildeburgh
Wiglaf, a loyal warrior
A Dancing Bear
Thanes, Earls, Warriors, Wenches, Monks, Water Nymphs, Jugglers, Acrobats, Old Crones, Dancers, Stable Girls
Speak / Sing Chorus, who may also play the above

NOTE: The parts of the Queen, Hammerfist, the Priest, Brunhilde and Wiglaf also may be played by members of the Chorus

The action takes place in the world of the Vikings

Period – the fifth century AD

MUSICAL NUMBERS

ACT I

Overture
1 Days of Doom   Chorus
2 The Feast at the Meadhall
   (a) Jugglers
   (b) Dancing Bear
   (c) Tumblers and Wrestling
   (d) Obe and Chorus
3 Long, Long Ago
4 Grendel
5 Departure of Grendel
6 My Name is Beowulf
7 Grendel, You Will Meet Your Match
8 Have You Seen My Mother?
9 The Approach of Grendel   Chorus
10 Finale. Free! *with* Wedding *and* Wedding
    March   Chorus

ACT II

11 Opening *and* Grendel's Mother
12 If You Could But Know   Beowulf and Hygd
   (a) Journey To The Dark Lake
13 When First We Met   Hygd
14 Descent *and* Sea Creatures Dance
15 Bingo Song
16 Yes, Once Again We Have Conquered   Chorus
17 The Passing Years (Symphonic Apotheosis)
18 Finale. The Fight With the Dragon: Funeral
    Music: Sub-Chorus of Monks: Eulogy:
    Dirge

The Music for *Beowulf* can be obtained from Samuel French Ltd

BEOWULF

Beowulf belongs to every modern English-speaking person or European as part of his heritage; it is the oldest surviving work of literature in the language of the common people from the lands which now constitute the E.E.C. *Beowulf*, says Michael Swanton, "is to English what the *Odyssey* and *Iliad* are to Greek".

The single manuscript now in the British Museum dates from about AD 1000 but the poem itself was probably made in the eighth century—and even then the story was several hundred years old, having been brought to England by the invading Angles. Who the original poet was, who copied the existing manuscript and why its edges are charred with fire are all unknown to us but it was obviously a popular story in Anglo-Saxon England as many a boggy place was nicknamed "Grendel's Pit" after the habitation of the grisly monster in the poem. Since the poem's rediscovery and printed editions in the middle of the last century the epic struggle between the brave Beowulf and the monsters has once again gripped the imaginations of thousands of people.

Beowulf was written in Anglo-Saxon which now has to be learned like a foreign language with a good deal of conjecture as to pronunciation. This should not deter anyone from producing this musical version because there are several excellent modern translations which are well worth consulting before embarking on a production. Michael Swanton's *Beowulf* (Manchester University Press, 1978) is a prose translation with many helpful notes. Michael Alexander's verse translation (Penguin, 1973) is an exciting and accessible version and Ian Serraillier has made a stimulating verse edition for young people in his *Beowulf the Warrior* that should whet the imagination of any potential cast (Oxford University Press, 1954).

Entertainment in Anglo-Saxon England certainly involved the telling and singing of fantastic stories of adventure and bravery in which humans mixed with heroes of superhuman strength in a world inhabited by giants and monsters—a world made popular again by Tolkien. There is an evocative description of how *Beowulf* might first have been performed in the Quennells' *Everyday Life in Anglo-Saxon Times* (Carousel Books, 1972).

The Setting

Although *Beowulf* is an Anglo-Saxon story it is set in the fifth-century world of the Vikings. It was a violent and terrible time in some respects and it is no accident that the word "berserk" was first used to describe the fury of Viking Warriors or that one of their tribes was the Vandals! But the various discoveries of treasure-hoards such as the Sutton Hoo burial and a good deal of recent interest in Viking travel and art have shown that these people had a rich culture—and they placed a great deal of importance on live entertainment: wrestling, great feats of juggling and gymnastics, lewd limerick writing competitions, horse fighting and drinking together with the singing of minstrels passed away the long evenings of the Scandinavian winter.

The age in which the poem is set was, as far as the Vikings were concerned, pre-Christian but the *Beowulf* poet, obviously a believer himself, makes his characters familiar with the Bible and it is certainly possible to interpret the whole poem as an allegory.

Reference to maps of Northern Europe in the sixth century will show the various countries involved in the saga and visits to museums (especially in York or London) or a study of illustrations of Viking shields, sword-hilts and brooches will provide interesting ideas for costume design while a particularly colourful picture of Viking life is provided in *The How and Why Wonder Book of Vikings* by Brenda Lewis (Transworld, 1975) or by Peter Brent in *The Viking Saga* (Weidenfeld and Nicolson, 1975). We need hardly stress how helpful it is to acquire a flavour of Viking times and to secure the interest and co-operation of colleagues in History and Art if this show is attempted in a school or college.

Words and Music

Beowulf is a very long poem; much of its detailed description has to become visual, much of its narrative turned into action, most of its verbal exchanges transformed into dialogue in order to make a stage musical. It also needed extensive pruning to fit the whole into a two-hour show. Some characters have disappeared and others have been invented in order to achieve the required blend of action, humour, excitement and romance. Anglo-Saxon verse did not rhyme but it had strong alliteration and a rich vocabulary: we have attempted to exploit these qualities in this version and we hope, for instance, that producers and performers will respond to the pounding alliterations of the opening lines:

> Days of doom and desperate darkness
> Dismal dawns and terrible nights.

To create the lyrics of a modern rock-musical we have also introduced rhyme but how we have tried to reproduce the spirit of the original can be illustrated by the way in which we have adapted the words which close the poem and given them to the single girl singer to sing as a lament over the body of the dead hero.

The original Anglo-Saxon reads:

> cwædon þæt he wære   wyruldcyninga
> manna mildust   ond monðwærust,
> leodum liðost   ond lofgeornost.

Swanton's prose translation: "they said that among the world's kings he was the gentlest of men and the most courteous, the most kindly to his people and the most eager for renown".

Alexander's verse translation:

"they said that he was of all the world's kings
the gentlest of men, and the most gracious
the kindest to his people, the keenest for fame".

Our version for this musical:

Of all this world's kings, this man he was the best,
Kindest to his people's need,
Gracious, noble, free from greed.
Sing of his great strength and wisdom,
But above all else remember if you can,
He was a kindly man.

Our music too, though in the rock idiom, goes back to very early sources for its inspiration. It is built around the *Dies irae* (Day of Wrath) plainsong melody of the ancient Church and the cast will enjoy spotting how often and in what guises the tune returns

The Rock Musical

Beowulf as a rock musical is not, however, simply an exercise in archaeology. Its themes: the struggle against violence, vandalism and darkness, the stupidity in assuming that affluence brings real security or satisfaction, are as relevant today as ever. Furthermore the story abounds with grotesque characters who translate easily into a modern idiom, tremendous fights and a type of singing and dancing that pulsate with all the vitality of a disco. The Viking blend of sheer energy and raw humour, hero-worship and action are as familiar to the theatre, the football terraces or the rock concert as they were to King Hrothgar in his great drinking hall of Heorot —why not join him there?

Suggestions for Further Reading

"The Monsters and Beowulf" in *The Anglo-Saxons* ed. Peter Clemoes, (Bowes and Bowes, 1959).
"Beowulf the Headstrong" in *Anglo-Saxon England* ed. Peter Clemoes, (Cambridge, 1972).
The Saxon Age. A. F. Scott (Croom Helm, 1979).
The Vikings in Britain. H. R. Loyn (Batsford, 1977).

K.W.P. & K.R.C.

ACT I

The stage has many levels, backed by a plain cyclorama. There are rostra in tiers, with a pit c

As the Overture music begins the stage is lit with an unearthly green. Strange and horrible shapes move in the shadows, ungainly silhouettes lope across the high places. There follows a ritual procession of cloaked and helmeted figures carrying great shields and banners. This is the Chorus, who wind their way to various places, with their backs to the audience. Suddenly they turn and sing

Music 1: **Days of Doom**

Thanes ⎫
Warriors ⎬ Days of doom and desperate darkness
Women ⎭ Dismal dawns and terrible nights,
                Evil stalks out in the forests
                Danger lurks on the heights.
                Mighty monsters creep from caverns,
                Giants ravage middle earth,
                Powers of Hell at war with goodness,
                Man must fight from his birth.
                Then a mighty king
                Does a wondrous thing,
                Builds a glorious feasting hall
                Hrothgar king of Danes
                With his mighty Thanes
                Comes to sit and drink here with us all.

Fanfare

  Hrothgar and the Queen enter

Hrothgar (*singing*) I am granted glory in battle
                Strong my shield and stout my sword;
                I have made a mighty mead-hall
                There to share my gifts with all.
                Boldly rear its high arched gables,
                See its doors of burnished brass,
                Banquets furnish full its tables
                This the age that ne'er shall pass.

The Chorus repeat the last four lines then sing

Chorus   Power brings peace, provisions, plenty,
                Golden dawns and gentle nights,
                Mystic songs sound in the forests
                Days of dreams and delights.

Monsters go back to their caverns
Giants sleep and trolls make mirth,
Powers of Hell are stemm'd by goodness,
Peace has come to the Earth.
We all know somehow
Life's much better now—
Hrothgar has restored our pride
Gone the bitter thorns
Flow the drinking horns—
Justice, light and love go side by side.

Hrothgar Call up the musicians and let the feastings begin!

The stage is full of activity

Trestle tables are brought in by Servants. Wenches enter with drinking horns and jugs and pour mead. Servants carry in hogs' heads and joints. Obe enters, followed later by the Minstrel

Music 2: **The Feast at the Meadhall**

Chorus Drink well, drink deep life's horn of plenty
Knock back life's cup and leave it empty
Take life's rich horn, you strong and twenty
Play it right well and make your entry.
Youth's green estate a passing bloom
Advance we all to death's dark gloom.
So come eat and drink all well befriended
Take this good mead and be contented.

This drinking song, with slight variations, is repeated after the "acts" which follow

Obe My Lords, Ladies, Thanes and Earls—make way for Fitela Fast Fingers and his jugglers!

Music 2A

The Jugglers enter to a "dance" tune

Chorus Drink well . . ., etc.
Come drown your cares their life is ended.
Troubles forgot are fastest mended.
Obe Make way for the incredible Dancing Bear!

Music 2B

The Dancing Bear enters and performs

Chorus Come try this ale here recommended
Life's simple pleasures are extended
Now eat and drink, forget your sorrow,
Life's here today but gone tomorrow.
Obe From the land of midnight sun—Offa and the acrobats.

Music 2C

A Gymnastic Team enters and performs feats of strength, agility and daring during the next dance tune

During a further dance the revelry becomes rauocus—games of bob apple, trials of ordeal with blindfolds—pigs' bladders, etc. A primitive dance wherein a woman tries to reach the centre of a circle of dancers emerges. Obe stirs them to greater exuberance all the while

Obe and the Chorus sing

Music 2D

Obe	Come one, come all
Chorus	Join the rev'llers in this hall
Obe	Eat, drink, dance, sing
Chorus	Now's the time to have a fling
Obe	All your cares are gone
Chorus	As the dance goes on and on
Obe	Let the music play
Chorus	And the she-wolf find her prey—hey, hey, hey, hey.
	Let us sing, let us sing—hey, hey, hey, hey
	Join the ring, join the ring
	Now.
Obe	One two three four
Chorus	Do not open every door
Obe	Five six seven eight
Chorus	Why's your lover always late?
Both	Can she sew and cook
Chorus	Wash a jerkin in the brook
Both	Hey, hey, hey got you!

This song continues antiphonally

Obe	Come now fill your glass
Chorus	Find yourself a comely lass
	Take her on your knee
	With your purse she will be free.
	Life's a passing game
	Join the ring and say your name
	Let the she-wolf find her prey—hey, hey . . . (*etc. as verse* 1)

Hrothgar (*quietening the exhausted company*) Now we have feasted well we must listen to our Minstrel.

Minstrel But my Lord, what is there left for me to sing about?

Hrothgar My Queen shall choose.

Queen Tell us how long, long ago—the Lord made the Earth
And how He made life upon its bright plains.

The Minstrel bows in obedience—the company sit enraptured and still while the Minstrel sings alone in the spotlight

Music 3: Long, Long Ago

Minstrel Long, long ago, before we came
God, He made the earth.
It was a void, an empty space.
There was no light in that dark place.

He made the sun, the silver moon
Her light to give.
The hills and vales, the ocean blue
He made it all, for me and you.
He then made plants and trees
Furnished them with limbs and leaves
Cold winds and summer breeze,
The spring, the fall.
All creatures great and small
Things that creep and things that crawl.
Fish, fowl and flesh He made them all, them all.

Man then was made, a perfect creature
So subtly made
He gave us pride and conscience true
He shapes our lives and guides us through.
Last man He gave a good companion
So sweet and grave.
A beauty rare with flowing hair
This woman was for man to care.
Who strews the night with stars
Fixes planets' plotted paths
Holds comets in His grasp—we know, we know.
Cold winds and rains may blow
Thunder, lightning, winter snow
Here, in our hearts we know—and so, and so
So long ago, He made it all, so long ago.

By the end of the song the whole company is asleep—only Hrothgar and his Queen remain awake

Hrothgar Your song has woven a web around our minds, Minstrel—we will also sleep now.

Hrothgar and the Queen exit

The Minstrel moves to the side of the stage to join the offstage Chorus

Minstrel So all men led a carefree life
But with the coming of the night came **EVIL**.

There is a great explosion of lurid light

Grendel enters—a punk-like character who almost crawls on over the rocks. He may have some revolting Companions

Music 4: **Grendel**

Grendel (*singing*) Hrothgar—you've got a lesson to learn!
We all have to suffer and now it's your turn!
You might think you're great, you might think you've
 won—
But I'll show you your troubles have only just begun.
Because—I'm evil.
I am evil
Stinking with evil
I am rotten right to the core.
Evil, evil, I am the devil
I kick kindness down on the floor,
Out of the door, don't ask for more,
Kick it to death Yeah!
Evil Grendel
Living in squalor,
All my body covered in slime.
My behaviour fills you with horror
I'm adept at violent crime,
Won't pay the fine
Do any time
Tell them to push off—Yeah!
I'm revolting, I'm disgusting,
I'm so negative I'll make you sick
I'm inviting your disliking
I am really thick
Da!

Grendel (*shouting*) What am I?
Chorus (*shouting*) Evil!
Grendel Are you positive?
Chorus Yes positive.
Grendel Am *I* positive?
Chorus No! Negative.
Grendel Right. I'm negative and full of hate. When I see pleasure I spoil it; if something's clean I soil it. (*With terrible laughter he paints "Grendel Rules OK" and similar slogans, then dashes out the brains of several warriors*)

Grendel makes off with one of the warriors over his shoulder

The Chorus and Minstrel sing together during the action

Music 5: **Departure of Grendel**

Chorus ⎱ Mad with rage the evil creature
Minstrel ⎰ Grim and grisly grasped his slaughter
Up and away he's fleeing, leaving the devastation—

The Lights fade up. The horizon becomes blue

But with daybreak all the horror, awful mayhem
Blood and murder, no more entertainment, only
lamentation—now.

Slowly the others awaken and gaze around the scene of desolation in disbelief

They carry out the dead. Hrothgar, the Queen and Princess Hygd enter and survey the chaos in despair

Hrothgar (*singing*) O God—this is a terrible hour
Evil returns with all its power—
Such murder and death all horror and worse
Who then will rid us of this dreadful curse.
Warriors (*muttering and running wildly among the audience*) Who will rid us of this curse, this curse, who will rid us of this curse, curse, curse!

A horn sounds

Watchman (*from high on the cliff*) Strangers have landed on our coast and are climbing the cliff path towards us.
All Who are they—find out who they are.

Beowulf and his Companions appear on the horizon

Watchman Strangers, I can see that you are warriors and that you have steered your long ship to our coast—I must now ask who you are.

Music 6: **My Name is Beowulf**

Beowulf (*singing*)	Who am I?
Chorus	Who are you?
Beowulf	I am the man you've been waiting for.
Chorus	Is he the man we've been waiting for?
Beowulf	Who am I?
Chorus	Who are you?
Beowulf	A slayer of ogres and giants galore.
Chorus	A player of trumpets and little more.
Beowulf	My name is Beowulf,

Brave and bold they call me Beowulf,
Young and old they know me,
Fearless in slaughter
I give no quarter
Monsters and such like I tear them apart.
You see I'm Beowulf,
Full of daring I'm called Beowulf of the strong arm,
I have fought many a campaign
And times again
I have won through with my sword and stout heart.

True in every battle, men they die like cattle,
Young and old and side by side.
Now I war on evil, darkness and the devil,
Grendel, soon you'll have to hide.

Chorus   True in every battle, men they die like cattle,
                 Young and old and side by side.
                 Now he wars on evil, darkness and the devil,
                 Grendel soon you'll have to hide.

Beowulf repeats the song then adds the following

                 Yes I am Beowulf, quick and keen for glory,
                 Beowulf, just believe my story now, Beo, Beo, Beowulf

Chorus (*at the same time*)

                 Yes he is Beo, Beo, Beo, Beo, Beo, Beo, Beo, Beowulf,
                 Beo, Beo, Beowulf.

*The Watchman comes down the cliff to Hrothgar. They consult in whispers
and the Watchman returns to Beowulf and his Warriors who, carrying great
shields and spears, form an impressive group on the cliff-top. Hrothgar
organizes his court and after the following speech there is a solemn ritual in
which Beowulf and Company prop up their shields and spears and enter the
presence of Hrothgar after a winding journey from the cliff*

Watchman My lord of battles commands me to tell you that he knows of
your great deeds and your ancestry—you are most welcome. You may
enter his presence in battle-gear and helmed—but your linden-wood
shields and battle-shafts must remain here.
Beowulf All health to Hrothgar! I am a kinsman of King Hygelac, prince
of the Geats. Although I am still young I have achieved many great
deeds and am thought of as a champion among my people. Your hall
and land are infested with that scourge Grendel I hear—rumours have
already reached us that this splendid hall must stand silent and idle in
the hours of dark. That is why I have come, most sovereign lord, these
men will tell you that with my grip I have crushed giants, sea-serpents
and monsters—why should I not fight this Grendel single-handed?
Hrothgar These are indeed brave words—but how am I to know if your
strength is what you boast of?
Beowulf I have the grip of thirty men.
All Thirty men!
A Wide-Eyed Girl You can grip me any time, darling.
Hrothgar Where is our champion Hunferth Hairylegs. Wrestle with this
man and try his strength.
Beowulf Will you not believe me! (*He snatches up a goblet or similar object
and crushes it in one hand*)
Girl Oooh, what a crush!
Hunferth (*obviously preparing for wrestling in his corner*) That doesn't
impress me—get ready for a fight.
Beowulf I will fight you with one arm only. (*He kneels and puts one arm on
the table, ready for "grips"*)
Hunferth You'll regret this. (*He lets out great bellows and groans as he grips
Beowulf's hand*)

The whole Court watches spellbound as Beowulf forces Hunferth's arm down three times and on the third pins him to the table

I submit, I submit!

Beowulf (*leaping on to the table*) Now let me show you that I have the grip of thirty men! Come, do not be cowardly—you must learn that Beowulf is no idle boaster.

Prompted by the Women, the Men line up opposite Beowulf and behind Hunferth until thirty are in a line or several lines. Obe organizes things and acts as referee—there is a roll of drums and much groaning and gasping but in the end Beowulf throws the whole line to the floor

Obe (*holding Beowulf's arm aloft*) The Champion!

All Our Champion!

Hrothgar I see, my friend Beowulf, that it is to fight for us and as a mark of kindness that you have come here. Come, sit at the banquet with us and drink a horn of friendship. To Beowulf!

All Beowulf the brave!

Hrothgar Never since I became a warrior have I handed over responsibility to any man—but now I give you charge of Heorot—to make safe this house of the Danes. And if you come out alive from this ordeal of courage there will be no want of liberality—and this will be my most precious gift to you; my only daughter, Princess Hygd.

Hrothgar takes Princess Hygd's hand and leads her to face Beowulf. They look into each other's eyes in silence before Beowulf takes and kisses both her hands

Music 7: Grendel, You Will Meet Your Match

Chorus (*dancing and singing*)
    Grendel, you will meet your match,
    This man will your plan dispatch.
    Bursting of sinew and crushing of bone,
    Yes this man will take you alone.
    Vile Grendel your hour comes
    Now against you the luck runs
    'Bye now to Mother, she'll soon find another
    So now you're all on your own.

Beowulf (*singing*) Fiend from hell they call you
    But this will appal you,
    Beowulf will be the bait.
    I'm anticipating all your devastating
    I'll be lying here in wait. Hey!

Chorus   Grendel in your filth and slime
    Soon you will run out of time,
    You will discover the strength of another
    And also a thing we call pain.
    No more cause for us to fear
    When you battle with your peer,

We'll celebrate as your bones we hear break
And you cry out for mercy in vain.
Beowulf No barbiturate
Can help to dissipate
The awful pain you're going to feel.
How it will surprise you when I pulverize you
When I grip you how you'll squeal.   Hey!

Hrothgar Brave Beowulf you have restored laughter to our hall. Now you must bend your mind and body to this task. You must watch over Heorot tonight.

All exit, Beowulf and Hygd last. They part reluctantly, and Beowulf is left alone for a moment before he goes off

Darkness, during which Grendel goes into the pit and mists begin to swirl from it. A murkish green light and sloshing sounds emerge. The Lights gradually reveal Grendel slopping mud and filth over himself and speaking in a voice like a "punk" Henry Cooper

Grendel Luverly, this is fantastic, the great smell of Brutal, I really pong now, cooew my feet stink beautiful. I could stay in this swamp all day—aah!

Grendel's Mother (*off, in a voice like old bagpipes*) Grendel! How much longer are you going to be in that bog!

Grendel All right, Mum, I'm just finishing me tea!

Grendel's Mother (*off*) How many times have I told you not to take your meals in the bog—especially when you will insist on holding food between your toes.

Grendel All right, all right! I won't be long. Blimey—my mother—have you seen her? (*He sings*)

Music 8: Have You Seen My Mother?

Well, have you seen my mother?
She's revolting, wiv 'er 'air in curlers
And 'er body odour
She's an iron constitution that can change quite quickly
If she gets upset or eats raw kidney.
But oh—I love 'er so—she is my ma
She's all I've got—Ah!
When it comes to me she'll tell you straight
I've got the lot—Yeah!
So if she's sometimes hasty
Or a trifle vi'lent
It's because she has been snubbed or told
Be silent.
But for this her temp'rament is plainly
What you'd call abrasive or a touch insane.
Yes singin' in the barf
I often do I like a larf

I slop and splash abart
And when I splash
I spill my marf—Yeah!

Grendel's Mother enters. She is a hideous woman with gaudy clothes and an improbable hairstyle—probably a chiffon head-scarf over curlers and huge slippers

Mother You've been in this flippin' hole quite long enough—you're just getting soft, lazing around here: you're supposed to be back down that drinking hall tonight getting me some more tasty, hairy warriors and all you can do is wallow around. And what's this terrible pong in here?

Grendel Mum, stop it, Mum—it's me body lotion.

Mother Body lotion—you wanna toughen yourself up a bit—it's no good stinking like a stagnant pond if you can't keep up your evil deeds, my lad.

Grendel Mum, just cut it out, will you. Please don't send me back down that place again. I got you about thirty blokes the other night.

Mother Thirty, what's wrong with you, do you think I'm losing me appetite? (*She starts belting him*) Evil can only survive on murder and horror—thirty is only a start. We've got to make it so that the night is never safe.

Grendel I've just got this 'orrible feeling.

Mother There's no room for feelings in this game!

Grendel All right, let me have me ears pierced then!

Mother What are you drivelling on about now?

Grendel You promised, you promised last Christmas, I could have me ears pierced.

Mother Oh for cryin' out loud, what's he on about—you're a pansy, mate—you're no son of mine—first you want your hair dyed green and red, and now you want pierced ears.

Grendel Mum, listen will you, I just wanna look tough. How can I stick safety pins and fings through me ear'oles if I aint got any 'oles to stick 'em through—I've just gotta *look* tough so I can *feel* tough.

Mother Oh, all right, if it makes you happy—anything for a quiet life. I'll get the blacksmith.

Grendel (*exploding*) What! I'm not having no blacksmith touching my ear'oles. It's a delicate operation.

Mother Delicate, since when have you been delicate! I thought you wanted to be tough.

Grendel Yeah, well most of me mates do each other with a bone needle or somefing.

Mother (*losing patience*) Hammerfist, come 'ere!

Hammerfist enters, a huge burly blacksmith with a horned helmet and an enormous hammer

Hammerfist (*in a voice like thunder*) Did I hear you call?

Mother Yes you did, this son of mine wants his ears pierced—see to it will you.

Hammerfist (*without emotion*) Ears pierced, I see, I'll just get the rest of my tools.

Hammerfist goes off

Mother Now get out of that bath. (*She gets Grendel in a "half-Nelson" or some wrestler's hold and pins him, yelling, to the ground*) You can have your heart's desire.

Grendel Ow! Stop it, get off!—(*Etc.*)

Mother And once you've been done you can get down to Hrothgar's disco double quick and get me some men!

Hammerfist enters carrying his hammer, an anvil or block and chisel

Hammerfist Right, put his ear on here—left ear first.

Grendel, still struggling, is pushed on to the block. There is a great ringing of steel as the hammer bashes an iron chisel into his ear lobe. He utters suitably horrific yells as the process is repeated

What's the matter—got earache, sonny?

Hammerfist laughs hideously as he goes off

Grendel is left panting on the floor

Mother Now get dressed!

Grendel slowly begins to clutter himself in "punk gear"—a leather jacket with "DAMNATION" in metal studs is supplemented by a variety of chains and leather straps

Voice (*off*) Grendel, you coming down the disco tonight? We could really rip the place up!

Grendel I'm coming, but I'm coming on me own. I'm just putting on me bondage.

Hrothgar, I'm going to get you tonight
I'm in the mood for a terrible fight,
See all my bondage of leather and chain,
You'll never live to see freedom again.

Grendel goes

Darkness. In the darkness the scene changes to the hall where Beowulf watches with his Warriors. The following action is played in slow motion in silhouette, so that huge shadows are thrown against the cyclorama

Music 9: The Approach of Grendel

The Minstrel and Chorus speak/sing together

Minstrel Gliding softly through the darkness
Chorus   In the shadows, filled with madness
              Where the watchers keeping
              Are they all asleeping?
              Except one, who waits in silence

Waiting for the coming violence
Of the foe's appearance
Then he must make the clearance.
Down the misty moorland stalking
Comes the Grendel softly walking
All on fire with hate and blood lust
To the hall drive on his needs must;
Now the monster, he draws closer
Can't you feel the air grow colder.
Beowulf be ready
Steel your nerve now steady.
Foul the air with his corruption
All intent on our destruction.

Grendel opens the door and appears. Bring up general lighting. He walks round the hall and stretches out his hand to attack

Beowulf suddenly grips his arm

Grendel (*struggling*) Agh!

Beowulf I tell you, Grendel, you will never have met on middle earth, a man with a harder hand grip than this.

Grendel (*bellowing*) Let me go, back to the darkness—let me go, back to the fen—to my lair.

A terrible fight with hideous noises ensues

Minstrel Fear entered into the hearts of the listening Danes.

Warriors Quick, we must help our Captain—keep him pinned there, Beowulf. (*They hack at Grendel with their swords*)

Grendel Keep off, you scum, no sword can hurt me.

Beowulf (*to the Warriors*) Leave off. (*To Grendel*) Then you must discover that of all men living in this world I am the strongest. Flesh and bone will fail you in the end.

Minstrel (*speaking like a commentator*) A fault in the fiendish frame showed. Shoulder muscles snapped, tendons tore, bone joints burst apart.

There is a terrible ripping sound as Beowulf pulls off Grendel's arm and shoulder

Grendel runs off, bellowing

Beowulf I have cleansed Heorot. (*He holds up the arm and hangs it above the throne*)

Cheers resound as the characters regroup

Hrothgar enters with his Queen and Princess Hygd during the singing of the following chorus

Hrothgar sits Beowulf on the throne. There is a procession of Men carrying gifts of shields and other rich treasures, and finally a ceremony in which Beowulf is joined in marriage to Hygd

Music 10: **Finale**

Men (*singing*)   Freemen we here stand together
Free from evil, free from fears
Free to eat and sleep in safety
Free to live out all our years.
Now we honour this great champion
Drink a toast to Beowulf—
Beowulf.

Women (*singing*) Free to live in peace and harmony
Free to plant and free to plough
Raise our children warm in happiness
Kill the goose or fatten the cow.
We pay homage to this great warrior
Drink the health of Beowulf—
Beowulf.

All (*singing*)   Free to build our land's prosperity
Free to laugh and love and smile
Free to sport and free to make music
Free from stress and free from trial
We salute this mighty hero
Life and health to Beowulf—
Beowulf.

Fanfare

Hrothgar Let the marriage begin.
Beowulf For such a prize a man would fight a dozen Grendels.
Priest (*singing*)   Do you, Beowulf, nephew of Hygelac
King of all the Geats,
Take Hygd to be your lawful wedded wife.
Beowulf (*singing*) I do, I do, I do.
Priest (*singing*)   And do you, princess Hygd, daughter of Hrothgar
The lord king of all the Danes
Take Beowulf to be your lord and lawful wedded
husband.
Hygd (*singing*)   I do, I do, I do, I do.
I love him yes I do, for all my life through
Yes, now and for always I will make his dreams
come true.
Beowulf (*singing*) I've won her now she's mine, such beauty rare and
fine,
I'll love her and I'll hold her and I'll make her dreams
come true,
I love her yes it's true, I do, I do, I do.
Hygd (*speaking over the music*) With this ring, I thee wed

Hygd and Beowulf kiss

Beowulf And with this ring, I thee wed.

Reprise of Love Duet

Hygd (*singing*) I love you, yes I do, for all my whole life through,
I love you now and always and for all my life through,
I love you yes I do, it's true, I do, I do, I do.
Beowulf (*singing*) I love you, yes I do, for all my whole life through,
Now and always I will keep you my life through,
I love you, yes I do it's true, I do, I do, I do.
Priest I now pronounce you man and wife.

Wedding march as they process

Chorus Free to live our lives together
Free to dance and free to learn
Feel the strength which comes with unity
Find support at every turn,
Now we celebrate this young woman
Married now to Beowulf
Beowulf.
Health to both of them, let them live strong in love
What a lovely day, now let the drinking start
Such a lovely day, come let the drinking start.
Though we'd like to stay
The wedding feastings call and we must leave you now.

The Curtain falls, leaving only the Minstrel before it. Behind it are sounds of distant revels

Minstrel (*speaking*) And Grendel, foul creature, fled to the fens with
failing heart,
To a den where death awaited him.
His strength ebbing, he had staggered slowly
Blood dripping, life oozing,
To the dark lake of doom, he dived
Into its icy waters. Hell had him!
(*Pause*)
Let us refresh ourselves and meet once more
In the great drinking hall!

The Minstrel goes, and Lights fade

ACT II

Darkness. All the Company except Beowulf, Hygd, Hrothgar and the Queen are sleeping after their banquet. Shapes are only dimly visible. Suddenly a spotlight comes up on Grendel's Mother

Mother You thought this saga had ended didn't you—you'd forgotten me, with all that ridiculous mead drinking and celebration—well, I'll tell you what I think of your saga—it stinks—it's Danish blue. My lovely boy is lying dead at the bottom of the lake and all I hear is singing and you lot drinking and stuffing yourselves! But big Mummy is here for REVENGE!

The warriors grab their swords, but she sings and moves so violently that they can't really get near her

Music 11

(*Singing*) I've a nasty disposition
        Evil of my own volition
        Spawned in sloth by mutant creatures
        Soon you'll see my finer features
        Puny weak humans your vile ablutions
        All your nice skin will feel my pollutions.
        I'll drink your blood and pop both your eyeballs,
        Tear out your heart and scatter your vitals.
        You killed my baby, now you'll discover
        All the fury of an injured mother.

        Should you hide or find protection
        I'm a dab hand at detection
        I'll hunt you through bog or byroad
        Soon I'll have your G.P.O. code,
        Just when you least would like me to visit
        I'll just drop by with manners exquisite,
        I'll break the doors and furniture maybe
        Strangle the cat and step on the baby
        You killed my baby—now you'll discover
        All the fury of an irate mother.

She holds all at bay and the action freezes

Minstrel So the monstrous ogress came to Heorot
             Where the Danes slept in the hall.

Mother (*to the Minstrel*) All right, you can call me names—but is won't stop me doing what I'm going to do. Here's a strong warrior, noted in battle are you? One of Hrothgar's favourites—a hero of the hall eh? You'll do in exchange for the life of my son. (*She falls on a strong warrior and carries him off over her shoulder*)

Mother exits

All (*with great wailing and gasping*) Beowulf! Where is Beowulf? Help us! Hrothgar. (*They run wildly around the stage and into the auditorium*) Evil has returned!

Hrothgar enters

Hrothgar The devil has come for revenge. We are helpless against this terrible scourge—our only hope is to turn to Beowulf—go to his chamber at once.
All (*chanting*) Doom and disaster, hell and destruction, desolation, DESOLATION!

Beowulf enters

Hrothgar (*sings to Beowulf*)
    Beowulf, once more to you we turn—
    Our hearts full of grief—with anger they burn—
    The Mother of Grendel has ravaged the hall
    One of our heroes has been first to fall.

He almost breaks down with grief

Beowulf You must bear your grief bravely—and your friend's death must be avenged—where does this monster live?
Queen (*singing*) She inhabits a strange region
                Of wild fells and windswept moors
                Treacherous tracks through boggy wastelands
                High upon lonely tors
                At the bottom of a dark lake, set about with twisted
                  trees.
                At a depth no man can suffer
                Lurks the ogress Grendel's Mother.
Hygd O Beowulf, you cannot go on such a dreadful journey!
Queen I am sorry at heart for your daughter—but daring is the food of fighting men and it is best that you accept it.
Beowulf (*tenderly holding Hygd*) Hrothgar, I can promise this. Grendel's mother will never protect herself by hiding in the darkest depths. For I shall seek and destroy her. But I undertake this with a heavy heart.
Hrothgar You must take our finest horse and arms for your great task.
Beowulf I shall be glad of your horse.
An Earl And you must take this bright and wonderful sword. Hrunting is its name—it has fought many battles and legend has it that it was fashioned on the anvil of the gods.

Beowulf (*taking the very heavy sword*) Thanks good friends—now I must ask you to leave us alone.

All withdraw slowly until Beowulf is left alone with Hygd

Hygd You seem determined to undertake this impossible task.

Beowulf I'm not sure that it is impossible—someone must be able to follow the monster to the bottom of the lake and kill her.

Hygd But why you? There are men who call themselves champions who drink mead at Hrothgar's table and yet it is you alone who must risk his life to make their lives safe.

Beowulf A hero must fight alone against evil.

Hygd Beowulf, I had hoped that you loved me more completely than to pose as a hero to me. It's not your strength or your daring that matter to me. Whatever your achievements in the past you *are* mortal, and now that you have made promises to me you must not take unnecessary risks.

Beowulf You are right to remind me of these things—underneath this veneer of confidence there are many uncertainties

Music 12: If You Could But Know

(*Singing*)   If you could but know all of my doubts and fears
How I've struggled down the years
Often hiding bitter tears.
It's not being strong that matters
But to oppose wrong and that is
What I do
And I must see it through.

Hygd (*singing*)   If I could but know all of the depths of your mind
What enigmas would I find
What strange qualities combined.
It's not people's words and chatter
But their real aims that matter
More to you,
And we must see this through.

Beowulf   There are no strange myst'ries to my mind,
It's not people's words and chatter,
But their real aims that matter more to me now,
And I must see this through.

Both   And we must see this through.

Hygd (*after a long pause*) Yes, you *are* right; but *please*, please be careful. I cannot bear to lose you so soon.

Beowulf You must come with me to the edge of the dark lake—but first I must select strong horses for our journey.

Beowulf exits

The Stable Girl, Brunhilde, enters carrying a bucket or bag of fodder— she wears a horned riding-helmet and riding-gear

Brunhilde (*putting down the bucket*) Really, the demands of these royal stables are quite horrendous. We've no sooner recovered from a week of horse fighting and now the king sends demands for steads with braided manes. These Danes and Vikings have disgusting habits—you should go to a horse-fight some day just to be nauseated! They get the fiercest stallions they can find—two of them—then they mark out an area on the ground, tie up a couple of mares so that the stallions start rivalling each other to gain attention—and they prod the creatures with sticks to get their tempers up. It's a revolting spectacle—the stallions rear up on their hind legs and flare their nostrils. And their owners get so excited they fight amongst themselves—all quite bestial. You read any book about the Vikings in future and it will say their principal vices were drinking and horse-fighting—you'll see—I find it very surprising that there's a royal interest in horse ownership these days—it seems to have become utterly debased! Breakfast time, chaps!

Simultaneously, two or three hobby horses poke their heads from the wings or are led on by other Stable Girls

Hildeburgh (*a lisping Stable Girl*) What's the task for today, Brunhilde dear?

Brunhilde Today we have a ROYAL visit. The king is sending his latest champion here to select a horse for some wild exploit. (*Noticing the meaningful glances of the girls*) Hildeburgh, he is coming to look at *horses!* This play is not *Equus!*

Hildeburgh O don't be so cross, Brunhilde—you must allow me my fantasies.

Another Stable Girl We all know about your fantasies darling—the last time we had a champion here choosing a horse it took you three hours to show him the hayloft.

Brunhilde Girls, that will *do*. We have to get this place ready for a royal guest. You know what importance the royal family attach to their horses and to good grooming—and if this man is a man of quality he will appreciate all the finer points—we must only show him the best models, none of the clapped out stuff we usually try to sell—now get down to it.

The Girls feed, wash down and groom the hobby horses, and actually pay more attention to their own grooming

Brunhilde exits. Beowulf enters behind Hildeburgh

Beowulf Health to you fair damsel!

Hildeburgh (*spinning round, flustered*) Oooh, health to *you*. I am afraid you have taken me unawares—er—who are you?

Beowulf My name's Beowulf. You may have heard of me—I believe I'm something of a myth already.

Hildeburgh (*winding one arm round his neck*) My name's Hilde—and I'm a miss too you know! (*She simpers and gazes at him*)

Brunhilde enters with a voice like thunder

Brunhilde Hildeburgh, put him down! Are you from the royal hall, from the court of King Hrothgar?
Beowulf Yes, I have come to select two fine horses.
Brunhilde Delighted to meet you. You have a splendid grip, I hear. (*She shakes his hand*)

Beowulf makes it obvious she is more than a match for thirty men

Welcome! Now, we have these . . . (*She reels off various horsey statistics*)
Beowulf (*looking at the horses' teeth, etc.*) These are magnificent steeds. Will you help me to mount?

The Girls fall over each other to help him on to a horse

And my wife shall ride beside me on this. Perhaps you will bring it behind me.
Brunhilde Gladly. *I* will do that.

Beowulf goes. Brunhilde rides out after him

Stable Girls Look at that—not a look backwards! *Men!*

Music 12A

The Stable Girls exit. As the Minstrel speaks the following over music, a procession winds its way up the cliffs to the edge of the pit: it includes Beowulf, Hygd, Hrothgar and Soldiers

Minstrel So they followed the tracks of the evil one
      Across the fog-shrouded moorland—then, leaving
      Their horses they scrambled up sheer rocks and
      Rough tracks—through desolate, uninhabited country
      Until at last, Beowulf suddenly saw the waters of the cheerless lake.
Beowulf The water is turbid with blood. This is where I must dive.
Hygd Not there, surely. Look at the water snakes and strange shapes which curl in the depths.
Beowulf They are not immortal. Watch! (*He takes a bow and fires into the water*)

The Soldiers fish out a strange monster with their boar hooks

Now I must prepare; bring me my arms.

The Soldiers give Beowulf a mail shirt, helmet and sword

Hrothgar This sword has never failed any hero in battle.
Beowulf Hrothgar, I dare not look behind in case my heart fails me—but if I do not return you must be father and guardian to all that is precious to me. (*He pauses only to kiss the hand of Hygd, to hold the arm of Hrothgar—then dives into the pit*)

Hygd turns away

The others go to comfort her, then go, leaving her alone

Music 13: **When First We Met**

Hygd (*singing*) When first we met, I knew at once,
                     A single glance, it was enough.
                     His noble head and clear eye
                     I felt my heart take wing and fly.
                     For such a man, for such a man, for such a man
                     A girl would die.
                     So now he's gone, here I remain,
                     One simple wish, a burning flame.
                     God help me now, what can I do,
                     Without this man my life is through.
                     To such a man, to such a man, to such a man
                     A girl is true
                     A girl is true.

Hygd exits slowly as the Lights fade

In the gloom the scene changes to represent an underwater cave. The light is green and watery with touches of blue and red—all the movements are slow and laboured or flowing as if being viewed from a glass sided swimming pool. Strange electronic sounds, like those heard in amusement arcades fill the air. In the centre is a sort of counter on which glittering Viking-like treasures— e.g. yoghurt cups with glass beads—are set up

> *Two Water-Nymph Girls with weed-draped swimming costumes float in wearing sashes which read "Viking Saga Holidays", they carry and set up a notice: "The Cavern—underwater amusements"*

Music 14

Watery music begins and there follows dance of water creatures. Mermaid-like Girls float around like "Legs and Co." but intertwined with great coils and tentacles

> *A group of Old Ladies enter with headscarves and sit on stools around the centre counter. Their chattering entry and awkward movements are in direct contrast to the grace of the previous dance. Words like "'Oo, me feet are killing me!" are heard in the hubbub. Grendel's Mother enters, takes a microphone and sits at the central counter as if she is about to run a bingo session*

Mother Right. Now, girls, let's see what fantastic prizes we have on offer today!

One of the two Water-Nymphs comes forward and speaks like the hostess of a T.V. show

Nymph We have here a magnificent bowl known as Sutton Hoo ware; encrusted with rich enamel—then we have this charming gold bracelet that once belonged to Eofor, the slayer of Ongentheow, son of Wonred, brother of Wulf, husband of Hygelac's daughter.

An Old Crone Oh, yes, fancy!

Second Nymph A superb shield, taken from Wulfgar, Prince of the Vandals, by Grendel—our dear departed friend.

Cheers, sounds of "Shame", "He was a lovely boy", "Ah!", etc.

Splendid workmanship. And lastly, our top prize for today—a stupendous sword—a giant sword of unknown age forged in a giant's forge—the wonder of its kind—yet so enormous that no known man can wield it. (*She gasps*)

Mother Now you've seen the prizes, eyes down!

Music 15: **Bingo Song**

(*singing*) On the red, Hrothgar's fate
　　　　　Thirty-eight.
　　　　　On the blue, Danish wench
　　　　　Twenty-two
　　　　　But what's this on the green
　　　　　Hrothgar's Queen—seventeen
　　　　　Oh yes one day soon I'll smash her little skull.
　　　　　On the red, devil's hive
　　　　　Nine till five
　　　　　On the green Grendel's tricks
　　　　　Fifty-six.
　　　　　On the blue, well look you
　　　　　Thatcher's den, number ten
　　　　　Yes, she and I are really quite good pals.
　　　　　On the blue, doing fine
　　　　　Sixty-nine
　　　　　Still on blue number two
　　　　　Sutton Hoo.
　　　　　On the green sweet sixteen
　　　　　Viking swine number nine
　　　　　Oh dear how I hate that nasty little lot.
　　　　　On the blue, death to you, eighty-two.
　　　　　Hate, hate, hate, number eight on the red
　　　　　Number three, look at me can't you see what I've got
　　　　　Oh, I've a certain something they have not.

She chants into the mike in an even more frenzied way until, by the end of the song she is completely berserk

　　　　　On the red stay in bed, sixty-five
　　　　　On the green, quite untouched, just thirteen
　　　　　Savage Picts, twenty-six, black and blue forty-two.
　　　　　And so now we really start to move it by

(*Faster still*)

　　　　　Number three, now bad luck always comes
　　　　　Like the wolf at the door forty-four.
　　　　　Ninety-nine, now you're mine

Forty-three don't you see
I hate your Anglo-Saxon poetry.
Now eyes down on the blue thirty-two
Rape and crime do your time twenty-nine
On the make forty-eight, on the blue, twenty-two
Why we must all make profit from the state.

During the following Beowulf swims in—preferably from above down a huge strand of water weed

King of tricks, politics, sixty-six
Take a dive on a bribe, ninety-five.
Forty-one, twenty-eight, human kind going straight
I hate oh how I hate yes HATEY HATE!

Beowulf Bingo!

Mother Who said that, who said that?

Beowulf There is one who is not afraid of you, vile thing! Now bid farewell to your life!

The Old Crones fly at him, but he drives them off with his sword; they clutch at him but at last he faces her

Mother Come at me would you? I can tell you now that stupid little sword won't help you. Ha, ha—I'll wrestle with you till there's not a bone left unbroken in your body. (*She laughs mockingly*)

Beowulf (*finding that the sword makes no impression on her*) Very well, I'll fling this useless thing away—my own strength will have to suffice me!

They wrestle—first he throws her but then she rolls on top of him and draws a knife. There is a desperate struggle in which he only just manages to force her arm back—he staggers to his feet and looks around for some help

Minstrel (*watching anxiously*) The sword, Beowulf, the great sword—you can wield it!

Beowulf siezes the great sword and swings it

Mother No, no, not that—ah! (*She dies hideously*)

Beowulf (*gazing at the sword*) All thanks to this wonderful blade. Now I must give it one more task—to hack off the head from Grendel's corpse and take it back for a prize. (*He does this*) The blade—it is melting like ice—the blood of Grendel is eating into the metal! I must leave this place and take nothing with me except the sword hilt and the head of Grendel. The blood that has been shed here was too hot, the fiend that died too deadly by far.

Beowulf exits

The Lights fade to a Black-out. In the darkness the others exit and the scene changes to a group of Warriors with Hrothgar and Hygd gathered anxiously round the "pit"

First Warrior There is more blood rising and marbling the surface of the water.

Second Warrior I fear there has been much terrible slaughter.
Third Warrior It is unlikely that we shall see our master again.
Hygd No, no, you must be wrong. He is wonderfully strong.
First Warrior Dear lady, we are seasoned warriors, experienced men. I am very much afraid that the she-wolf of the deep has done away with him.
Hrothgar It is now the ninth hour when darkness comes over the face of the land. All hope of our champion must be given up. I must turn my face homeward.

There is a movement of some of the Warriors but a few who wear Beowulf's emblem remain with Hygd

Loyal Warrior Wiglaf You may abondon the cliff top—but I will remain, sick at heart to stare into the deep.
Another Loyal Warrior I hope to see our beloved captain again—though I believe I shall not.
Hygd I must stay and watch with you.

A long silence

Wiglaf A helmet! A horned helmet! Beowulf is swimming to the surface!

Beowulf crawls out of the pit. They all rush to him and unfasten his armour. With one arm around Hygd he holds high Grendel's head, which is then stuck on a spear

Minstrel And they retraced their steps, light-hearted and bold, down familiar paths and entered again Hrothgar's hall.

This is represented by a procession

Beowulf Behold O King—these trophies from the lake mean but one thing —Victory!

Music 16: Yes, Once Again We Have Conquered

Chorus Yes, once again we have conquered
Yes, once again we've won thr-o-ough
We are the ones who will stand strong
Take it and yet we stay tru-u-ue.
We will stand to-gether
We will fight for ever
We will never never
ever let you down no no no.
Da dada da, etc.
No matter what they do
We will come fighting through
And we will all be true,
We'll stop them all for you
Here our pledge renew
It's one for all and all for you
No matter what they do
We will come fighting through

And we will all be true,
We'd stop the world for you
Let's hear one more call
It's all for one and all for you
We're all for you.

Music 17: The Passing Years

The words and actions are timed so that the next scene is ready to begin as the music finishes

Minstrel (*speaking as various symbolic actions are carried out*) You should have seen the gifts that were piled on Beowulf—treasures far more costly than those he left behind in the underwater cavern. And then, of course, they had a great feast—we're not going to show you that because you've seen one already—and you know what these Danes were like—they loved a saga, so Beowulf had to reel off his adventures with all the gory details—he went on and on—and then Hrothgar made a noble speech, and Beowulf made another speech. They concluded all sorts of peace treaties and non-aggression pacts. Then they embraced each other and made solemn vows—and embraced again—and although Beowulf promised to return and Hrothgar begged him to—they both had the uneasy feeling that they would not meet again on middle earth.

During the above they all make their way to the "cliff top". Beowulf and his company embark over the horizon, while Hrothgar and his company remain in silhouette. The sky turns from blue to darkness

Chorus (*speaking as the stage empties*)
Away went the boat over the foam flecked sea
Proud, curling prow cutting the waves.
Until they saw the great cliffs of the land of the Geats
And beached the longship safe on familiar shores.

In the darkness a throne is set up c, *and Beowulf, now grey-haired, sits in it. The Lights come up*

An Earl enters

Earl Health to Beowulf. For fifty years, bravest of men, you have ruled the kingdom of the Geats after the death of Hygelac. You people's love is unflinching and as a token of my loyalty I bring you this gold cup plucked almost from the dragon's mouth.
Beowulf (*taken aback*) Say again, where did you get this cup?
Earl My lord, I am an adventurer. I took it from the treasure hoard in the long barrow which foolish tradition says is guarded by a dragon.
Beowulf Tradition! It is true! That treasure has been watched over by a terrible dragon for the last three hundred years. You young men must learn restraint. The dragon's revenge will be fearful—it may already be too late.

A red light begins to flicker on the cyclorama. Distant cries of women become mingled with shouts of "Fire!"

From all sides Men and Women rush in and fall at Beowulf's feet, splutter-ing out that their homes are on fire. Among them enter a second Earl, Wiglaf and a Priest

Second Earl Mighty Beowulf, an evil one has come amongst us. Your great hall is on fire.

Above, in a lurid light, the laughing ghosts of Grendel and his Mother appear

Beowulf Bring me the largest shield in the kingdom. Old as I am, I will fight this creature.
Earls No, my lord, you must not.
Beowulf Do as I say. I am not so feeble that you can escape my strong right arm. Arm yourselves, you must come with me to the dragon's lair.

They cower away

What is this? Is this my shield ring of confidence?

The great shield is brought in

Now, who will come with me into the fire?

They all back away

Wiglaf My lord, I waited for you when you slew the she-monster. I will not forsake you now.
Beowulf Wiglaf, we will go together.

Music 18: **Finale**

The Lights fade until a red light rises from the pit. Beowulf and Wiglaf approach, with the others trailing. They are driven back—but, hiding behind their shields, they enter the pit. We see their swords whirling. Suddenly there is a terrible cry, and Wiglaf emerges—alone

Wiglaf The dragon is dead—but our master is terribly wounded.
All Look, he comes.
Beowulf (*staggering out of the pit*) I have fought my last battle. Who will take up this sword?

They flinch away

Will no-one take up the sword? Will no-one rid the world of corruption? (*He dies*)
Priest Our great lord is dead. We must honour him as befits a champion.

Slowly the whole cast assemble to build a pyre, on which all arms and helmets are placed and around which shields and banners are stood

Hooded Monks enter and chant

A ring of Warriors encircles the pyre, and when everything is in position the body of Beowulf is placed on top

Chorus (*as the pyre is built*)

> Now our world returns to darkness
> Dismal years and dark despair
> Foul corruption stalks unhindered
> Evil leaves its lair.

The body is carried very slowly

> Ignorance and superstition
> Thirst like wolves at every door
> Hawk and crow now fly together
> Hunger drives men from the law.
> Fifty years of peace and plenty
> Gone with history's closing door.

Sub-chorus of Monks Requiem aeternam, requiem aeternam,
Dona eis domine et lux perpetua.

Chorus

> Soon will end our cultured nation
> With the death of him our sage
> Now begin your lamentation,
> History's darkest age.
> To the east the scourge of reason,
> Vandals, Goths and Mongol Horde,
> Who will stem the great invasion,
> Who take grasp the warrior's sword?
> Now an end to civilisation,
> Bloody death soon our new lord.

Monks

> Dark are the days of the deaths of heroes
> Strong our lament for this great man—
> Live now in legend, his strength still with us
> Laughter and grief must not sound again.

Full Chorus

> Brave Beowulf is now at rest
> Evil will soon return again
> Who then will tread the champion's path
> Where shall we find him and what is his name?

The chorus is repeated, by which time the body is on the pyre

Monks

> Requiem aeternam, dona eis domine
> Et lux perpetua

A Warrior walks forward and lights the pyre. There is a great shout as the pyre lights

All Ah!

Eulogy

A single Girl Singer comes forward

Girl

> Of all this world's kings, this man he was the best,
> Kindest to his people's needs, gracious, noble, free from greed.
> Sing of his great strength and wisdom,
> But above all else, remember if you can
> He was a kindly man.

The Chorus repeat while the Girl sings

Chorus   He was a rather quiet man
            I used to know him fairly well
            He had a kind word for everyone he met—
            No matter who—
            He'd make you feel at home
            With just a word or two
            Remember him as I do
            That he was a kindly man.

Warriors do a ritual walk around the pyre as the Chorus continue

            Beowulf is dead
            Darkness comes again:
            Gone is our great Lord
            Darkness comes again:
            Who'll take up the sword?
            Has he died in vain? Was it in vain?

The Lights fade to a Black-out, as—

                        the CURTAIN *falls*

FURNITURE AND PROPERTY LIST

ACT I

On stage: Rostra
Central pit. *In it:* leather jacket with chains and straps (preset for **Grendel**)

Off stage: Shields, spears, swords **(Chorus, Warriors)**
Banners **(Chorus, Warriors)**
Trestle tables, hogs' heads, joints, stools **(Servants)**
Drinking horns, jugs of mead **(Women)**
Juggling items **(Jugglers)**
Bob-apple games, blindfolds, pigs' bladders **(The Company)**
Paint **(Grendel)**
Large hammer, anvil or block, chisel **(Hammerfist)**
Detachable "arm" **(Grendel)**
Throne (set during action)
Various gifts of shields, rich treasures **(Men)**
Wedding ring **(Beowulf)**
Wedding ring **(Hygd)**

ACT II

On stage: Remains of banquet on tables, etc.
Heavy, bright sword
In pit: monster, **Grendel's** "head"
(Optional) Huge strand of seaweed (in underwater scene)

Off stage: Bucket or bag of fodder **(Brunhilde)**
Hobby horses **(Stable Girls)**
Buckets, horse brushes, fodder **(Stable Girls)**
Bow and arrow **(Beowulf)**
Boar hooks **(Soldiers)**
Mail shirt, helmet, sword **(Soldiers, for Beowulf)**
Notice: "CAVERN—UNDERWATER AMUSEMENTS" **(Water Nymphs)**
Counter with treasures, including ornate bowl, shield, giant sword (set by **Company** during action)
Stools **(Old Crones)**
Microphone **(Grendel's Mother)**
Knife **(Grendel's Mother)**
Throne (set during action)
Gold cup **(Earl)**
Great shield **(Warriors)**
Materials for pyre **(Company)**

LIGHTING PLOT

Property fittings required: nil
An open stage

ACT I
To open: Darkness

Cue 1	(As Overture begins) *Fade up unearthly green light, shadow and silhouette effects*	(Page 1)
Cue 2	**Hrothgar** and **Queen** enter *Bring up general lighting to full*	(Page 1)
Cue 3	At start of **Minstrel**'s song *Fade to ¼, with spot on* **Minstrel**	(Page 3)
Cue 4	**Minstrel:** ". . . coming of the night, came EVIL " *Cross-fade to explosion of lurid light*	(Page 4)
Cue 5	**Chorus/Minstrel:** ". . . leaving the devastation." *Cross-fade to general lighting with blue on horizon*	(Page 5)
Cue 6	After general exit *Fade to Black-out, then bring up green light from pit, followed by general fade up*	(Page 9)
Cue 7	**Grendel** exits *Fade to Black-out, bring up silhouette effect on cyclorama*	(Page 11)
Cue 8	**Chorus/Minstrel:** "All intent on our destruction." *Bring up general lighting*	(Page 12)
Cue 9	As CURTAIN falls *Fade to spot on* **Minstrel**	(Page 14)
Cue 10	**Minstrel:** "In the great drinking hall!" *Fade to Black-out*	(Page 14)

ACT II

To open: Very dim shadowy lighting

Cue 11	After CURTAIN up *Bring up spot on* **Grendel's Mother**	(Page 15)
Cue 12	**Mother:** ". . . big Mummy is here for revenge!" *Increase general lighting*	(Page 15)
Cue 13	As **Mother** exits *Increase general lighting further*	(Page 16)
Cue 14	**Stable Girls** exit *Cross-fade to sinister lighting, favouring pit*	(Page 19)

EFFECTS PLOT

ACT I

Cue 1   After **Grendel** enters pit   (Page 9)
          Mists swirl from pit: "sloshing" sounds

ACT II

Cue 2   Scene changes to underwater cave   (Page 20)
          Strange electronic sounds